HOW TO MANAGE YOUR FINANCES

AT ALL TIME

(FREE FROM FINANCIAL WORRIES)

RICHARD J. HATCHER

Copyright © 2024 Richard J. Hatcher

All rights reserved. No part of this publication may be reproduced, distributed, or transmitted in any form or by any means, including photocopying, recording, or other electronic or mechanical methods, without the prior written permission of the publisher, except in the case of brief quotations embodied in critical reviews and certain other noncommercial uses permitted by copyright law.

TABLE OF CONTENTS

PART ONE
HOW TO HAVE BETTER SPENDING HABITS & LEARN PERSONAL BUDGET PLANNING

PART TWO
HOW TO AVOID DEBTS

PART THREE
HOW TO PAY OFF DEBT FAST AND MANAGE YOUR MONEY BETTER

PART FOUR
START INVESTING

PART FIVE
HOW TO BUDGET FOR RETIREMENT

PART SIX
HOW BEST TO SAVE

PART SEVEN
LIVE YOUR DREAM LIFE

PART ONE

HOW TO HAVE BETTER SPENDING HABITS & LEARN PERSONAL BUDGET PLANNING

Imagine a world where you can take that perfect holiday, pay for the kiddies' council, and give outrageously to people in your community. It's a nice pipe dream, is it not? The good news is that it doesn't have to stay a pipe dream. Changing many of your spending habits can put you on the fast track to turning those what-ifs into reality.

Your Money Classroom
This is how to relate to the way you learned about money growing up. Believe it or not, you picked up on a lot, whether it was designed or tutored to you or not. Was your family economical or frivolous? How much did your parents talk about money? Was giving a precedence in your ménage? Your money classroom has surely impacted your mindset around the money moment

Your Personality
As we look at our money classrooms, keep in mind that we're all wired differently. Our heartstrings, fears, and dreams are different. Indeed if you had siblings who grew up in the same house, and indeed if you had analogous external behaviors, the way you perceived and internalized those behaviors can be veritably different. This is why you may have veritably different money habits than your other family members. If you want to dig into your money personality.

The media and culture
We're bombarded with thousands of advertisements on a diurnal base. The companies who want us to buy their stuff produce advertisements in such a way that makes us feel like we aren't good enough until we've got their thing. And our musketeers won't suppose we're good enough unless we prove we've all the effects — the perfect home, the dream holiday, the matching Christmas pajamas on Instagram, right? This imaginary standard of living we hold everyone to in our culture has gotten way out of control.

SPENDING HABITS TO BREAK INCONTINENTLY

There are five common spending habits you need to break if you want to make your dreams reality

• Spending without a plan
Your money will vanish, and you won't know where it went If you don't have a yearly budget. You'll be like the average American beggar. Too numerous people live on further than they make and use credit cards to cover the difference. But when you have a plan in place to live on lower than you make and save for a stormy day, you're ahead of the game.

• Paying for convenience
I'm as shame faced as anyone of running through the drive-thru at Chick-fil-A because it's easy (and also, like, so great). But when we're paying for convenience all the time, we're letting money slip between our fritters. So, stop and take the time to consider the occasion cost of all those blind feasts!

• Spending without keeping a record

Losing track of the money you've spent or payments you've listed will ultimately come back to suck you, so let's break this money habit ASAP. Don't worry, you presumably don't need to whip out a pencil and go to the city on your checkbook tally.

• Making impulse purchases

You presumably know impulse deals are bad news for your bank account. Americans spend over 3,300 on impulse buys every time! 1 We frequently impulse-steal particulars like food, apparel, and indeed buses. Before you snare arbitrary effects that are not on your shopping list, ask yourself if you really need it... or indeed want it!

• Spending to feel more

This is called emotional spending If you tend to hit" add to tote" in a moment of retail remedy to forget your problems. The utmost of us have been ashamed of it at one point or another. I mean, when the effects are hard, it feels good to just dull the stress and spark some joy with a little shopping, right? But that megahit of happiness won't last. However, stay focused on your pretensions without letting passions get in the way!

HOW TO BREAK BAD SPENDING HABITS

Making many good opinions over and over will set you up for long-term success. So now that you're apprehensive about which spending habits have got to go, rather than what to apply rather.

Get on a budget
Give every bone a name at the morning of the month — and pay yourself first. Without savings to cover an emergency, your fiscal security is at threat, and You'll be tempted to use a credit card when the auto breaks down.

Understand yourself and your provocations.

Every single day, you have the power to make opinions that will move you forward financially or set you back. Knowing your strengths, trouble spots and tendencies is crucial to using them to your advantage. I'll educate you on how to get unstuck from your old money habits in my new book, Know Yourself, Know Your money.

Mess plan

Plan your reflections at the launch of each week to avoid paying an arm and a leg for fast food throughout the week. And when you do eat out, suppose doubly before you add on an appetizer or a drink.

Wait before you buy

Grown-ups learn to say no to themselves to gain less in the long run — anyhow of their current feelings or what everyone differently is doing. It takes wisdom to make opinions grounded on what will drive you forward, and it takes courage to put blinders on to what other people suppose. One question I frequently need to ask myself is, Would I buy this if no one ever sees it?

PART TWO

HOW TO AVOID DEBTS

We understand, then at PayPlan, that debt is an everyday part of life. After all, without debt products similar to mortgages numerous of us would be unfit to enjoy a home, and for those who attend university, a student loan is a necessary requirement.

Manageable debt can help us to live happily. When debt gets out of control or unanticipated changes impact your finances, the problem can take over your life. That's why we must understand what to do, to put ourselves in the stylish place to avoid debt and continue living life without solicitude.

This companion from PayPlan breaks down everything you can do to reduce your liability of falling into problem debt and how to cut back on everyday charges to free up further monies for your important savings buffer.

Plan for the unanticipated

Life has a habit of throwing a windfall, which is a crucial reason why numerous people find themselves in fiscal difficulty.

Whether it's losing your job or having to take time off work due to illness, you can prepare ahead. Some physical and internal health difficulties have the eventuality to be life-changing, so planning for these and seeking help as snappily as possible when they do, could have a positive impact on your whole life.

To avoid getting into unanticipated unborn debt, produce a savings buffer with any fat you have – aim to save up to at least three months' worth of income in an emergency fund as part of your future-proofing plan.

Assign a small quantum of plutocracy in your budget to transfer into a savings account each month, If you're suitable. You'll be amazed at just how snappily the aggregate can reach a significant quantum. This money can also be set away for emergency situations or big events in the timetable, similar to Christmas or birthdays.

We understand that numerous people may not have a great deal of disposable income after their bills have been taken out, but take 10 a month, for illustration

Top up your savings without having to suppose about it by setting up a standing order to transfer a set quantum each month into your savings regard. Only do this if you feel confident that you can go through with it – or ensure you can pierce your savings and withdraw monies as and when demanded.

Unborn proofing your finances for those big mileposts

Having a savings buffer allows you to plan and ensure those big life moments are covered – especially if they come along suddenly.

A new baby, marriage, buying a home, changing your job – all of these can be supported by this savings buffer if an exigency expenditure arises at the same time, allowing you peace of mind while avoiding debt and enjoying these milestones.

Find ways to cut costs

Cutting back on everyday charges can free up money to be saved. There are many effects you can attack first. Switch energy suppliers – a commodity as simple as moving electric and gas suppliers can save you hundreds of pounds every time on your bills. Try a cheaper supermarket – Give a budget supermarket a go, as they're known for their lower prices.

Check you have been allocated the right council duty band – numerous people pay too much for their council duty, so double check you're in the right band. However, which you may be suitable to set aside as savings, If you aren't you may be due a refund.

Cancel gratuitous subscriptions – If you don't use your Netflix account or infrequently visit the spa but still pay a class figure, also cancel these and save a little redundant cash.

Avoid takeaways and eating out unnecessarily – Try cuisine from scrape and buy particulars in bulk that can stretch across a variety of delicious reflections. Walk or bike when you don't need to drive – Cut down on the cost of energy and get some exercise in at the same time.

Challenge renewal costs for insurance – It's likely if you call your supplier and ask for a better deal they'll find a way to blink your price to keep you as a client.

Maximizing your savings

Check if it's delivering a stylish return on your money If you have a savings regard. There are a huge variety of savings accounts available that can help you put money down and save for a stormy day

Easy access savings accounts Allow you to pierce your money incontinently and withdraw it when demanded. They're handy for extremities, as numerous come with a card to give you access to cash at ATMs or over the counter at the bank.

Cash ISA Offers duty-free interest. There's a limit of 20,000 that you can put into these accounts and the interest you get is generally higher than normal savings.

Regular savings regard If you want some discipline when putting away money, these savings accounts limit the number of recessions you can make per time. They also limit how important you can transfer each month, but frequently offer better interest rates than easy-access savings accounts.

Avoid gratuitous purchases

If you can not make an unnecessary purchase – similar to an all-inclusive summer vacation – without credit. The stylish way to get those big effects we want is to simply save money for the purchase, by setting a realistic thing and working towards it.

When it comes to leaves, numerous trip agents offer an installment payment option that doesn't bear a credit deal and avoids you demanding to use a credit card or overdraft to cover the cost. This can be a real help, so look out for this if you're shopping for a vacation.

Budget effectively

Budgets are important when you're trying to manage your money effectively and avoid debt. They ensure all of your important charges are covered so that nothing is missed or paid late, while also leaving some spare cash for savings and extremities.

Try out the 50/20/30 rule

Some people find that the 50/20/30 rule works best for them. This means 50 of your income goes towards essential living charges including your mileage bills, rent or mortgage, food shopping, and energy.

20% of your income is put towards fiscal pretensions, similar to savings and making disbursements on any debts that you may owe, identical to a credit card or a hire purchase loan for your auto.

30 is left for disposable income, so you can use this to buy effects like little treats similar to cinema tickets or new clothes. You don't have to spend this whole 30, of course, so whatever is left over at the end of the month can be added to your 20 budget!

You can change and change these probabilities as you see fit – we understand that not everyone will have 30 left after their bills and other necessary charges have come out – but creating a set structure can help ensure all your costs are covered.

Find a way to keep track

You could also start to keep a spending journal – either on a tablet or on a spending tracking app.

There are a wide variety of apps available, some link automatically to your bank accounts, while others allow you to input your deals manually. There are some exemplifications of bones you can download and try out

Avoid finance deals where possible

'Buy now pay latterly ' deals and 0 interest offers can be enticing, allowing you to get your hands on a big purchase similar to a lounge or laptop incontinently, without any outspoken expenditure. A lot can happen in that six-month period that could affect you making disbursements.

It's easy to set these deals up and also forget about them altogether. This can lead to missed payments and a knock-on effect on your credit standing further down the line. Put a plan in place to ensure you can surely go make yearly disbursements later If you do wish to use one of these deals. However, saving until you can go the particulars and paying up front, is generally the safer option, If not.

Don't use credit when you have cash

It may be tempting to keep what's formerly in your bank account put away and to use a credit card rather, but if you spend that money away and don't have a way to make disbursements on what you've espoused, you could find yourself in some trouble.

Avoid using credit to pay for everyday purchases – unless you're working on rebuilding your credit standing, If you have cash in the bank. In which case, have a strict plan of what you can use it for – similar to when paying for energy or daily food shopping. Aim to pay off your full credit card balance every month, to avoid interest accumulating.

Ensure you understand all the terms and conditions

Before subscribing to any credit agreement or using credit, take the time to read the terms and conditions. It may feel like an onerous task but there may be a reference to freights and charges that could catch you out later down the line, or information about interest rates that could impact your capability to make your disbursements in full. ensure you completely understand the limitations and rules around any credit products you have to avoid issues later.

Look for better deals on big purchases

To avoid spending further than you can go on big purchases, shop around to find the stylish deal. Cheaper deals can frequently be set up online, or by staying for peak deals similar to Boxing Day or on Black Friday. Cheaper druthers in former models or last season's colors could also be a star buy, with considerable savings.

Check your duty law is correct

Your duty law is set by HMRC but it's your responsibility to check this regularly to ensure it's correct, and that you're paying the right quantum of duty. If you're underpaying this can be expensive and HMRC may communicate with you to ask that you pay back what you owe. Check your rearmost pay envelope slip for your law, also use the Gov.UK website to check what law should be applied to you.

You can set up a prepayment plan via your stipend, so that they take a little further than they generally would each month. If you find you're formerly underpaying you can't go to make up the difference in one full payment.

Make disbursements on time

Setting up a direct disbenefit for bills and credit products is the easiest way of ensuring your disbursements are made on time and in full. ensure the direct disbenefit is planned on a date when you feel confident there will be monies in your account.

We recommend assigning your payment date to two or three days after your usual allocated payday. This ensures there's a plenitude of time for monies to arrive in your bank account and any issues can be remedied before the bill date. So, if you're paid on the veritably last working day of the month, assign your bill payments to come out on the 3rd or 4th of the following month.

Making disbursements on time and in full ensures you don't have to deal with fresh freights and charges that can snappily increase the debt you owe and beget you bigger issues.

Limit how numerous credit cards you have

For some people, if they've more than one credit card, it can feel hard to keep track of how important it is and to which company.

It's better for your credit standing to avoid having a large quantum of credit available that you aren't using. However, similar to a mortgage or a home enhancement loan, implicit lenders may feel nervous seeing available credit sitting there that you aren't using If you need to apply for credit in the future. This is because if you decide to adopt it all at an afterpoint, it could put their disbursements at threat.

Also cancel these, If you have any credit cards you don't owe money and don't need them. Simply get in touch with the company they've been arranged through and ask that they shut down your account.

Pay off the balance on your credit cards

Set up a memorial each month to pay off the balance on your credit card at the end of every month. This will ensure the quantum owed doesn't steadily creep up and allows you to keep a handle on your borrowing. It's also great for your credit standing as it proves you can adopt a money and pay this reverse regularly and in full.

Only adopt what you know you can go with

Numerous people use a credit card to ameliorate their credit standing, adopting small quantities and repaying this reverse in full every month, to prove they can manage money. By using credit and icing you have enough to repay it in the same month, you don't fall into large quantities of debt.

Don't subscribe to a credit card just for prices

Lots of credit card companies are now offering prices and cash back on purchases made using their cards – and while a field Chesterfield pass or 5 worth of Nectar points sound like soliciting offers, ask yourself whether it's worth the original cost and conditions. As you're frequently incentivized to spend further money to gain these extras, it's too easy to find yourself in debt.

Ensure your overdraft is authorized

Ensure it's agreed with your bank If you feel that your current yearly spending may cause you to dip into your overdraft. This means you'll be allowed to adopt up to a certain quantum and a small figure will be charged per day until it's paid off.

Dipping into an unauthorized overdraft can be veritably expensive and lead to debt problems. The charges could indeed exceed the quantum you've gone over by, adding to what you need to repay to get back into the black. freights vary per bank but generally an unauthorized overdraft will charge around£ 1 to 6 per day or £ 5 to 35 a month.However, ranging from 10 to 25, which can snappily add up, If the overdraft is used for direct disbenefit payments a charge will be applied to each of these.

Flashback, an overdraft should only be used in an emergency situation. Speak to your bank if you need an extension if you know you're going to run over when making payments.

Avoid debt connection

Numerous people try to shift their debts around to avoid interest and Avoid debt connection, innumerable people try to shift their debts around to avoid interest and freight, especially when they're using credit cards. Debt connection can beget bigger issues latterly, as you discover the larger debt quantum means larger freights and interest charges. This can put a strain on your capability to make disbursements.

Consider life insurance and critical illness cover

Consider adding critical illness cover, If you can go with life insurance. This can ensure you're defended for the future in case you fall terminally ill or cannot work due to illness.

This type of cover can help pay your mortgage and bills and cover you and your family from debt if you're unfit to work. Protect around to find a good deal with a cover provider.

PART THREE

HOW TO PAY OFF DEBT FAST AND MANAGE YOUR MONEY BETTER

How to manage debt during a recession

With an implicit recession brewing and numerous Americans floundering to cover yearly charges, it can be delicate to decide whether to concentrate on erecting your savings or trying to pay down high-interest debt before the frugality gets more unstable.

The answer depends on your current fiscal stability. However, you should prioritize paying down high-interest debt, If you're financially secure and have emergency savings. This is especially true if you have a loan or line of credit with variable interest rates.

Go through your budget order by order. If you have anything you can part with now — like a redundant streaming service or a spa class you infrequently use — nix it.

Don't stop there, however. Make a list of places where you could gauge back if demanded. Are you shopping at the nicer grocery store in your area? Have you been getting gas at the accessible- but- more-precious pump? Flag places where you could make cuts if the effects get tough. Knowing you can acclimate your budget gives you two effects: an action plan and the peace of mind that comes with it.

Look for fresh work if possible

While severance rates continue to stay low, a brewing recession means companies will probably start making cuts. As with your budget, look for ways to develop a plan B then.

That could mean starting a side hustle or picking up many shifts at an original retailer or eatery. Sock away that redundant money to help pad out your savings or apply it to your payments if you have high-interest debt.

Immaculately, nothing will be with your current employment. However, having another income sluice in place can help you stretch your emergency fund further if commodity does. And if a recession does come in full force, competition for these redundant gigs will increase. Get a bottom in the door now.

Do whatever you can to make the minimal payment

Making your debt payments should be your top precedence, right over there with keeping yourself housed. However, your credit score takes a megahit, If you don't.

That means adopting money in the future will get more precious.

First, don't let yourself miss a payment because you simply forgot. Set up a memorial system for yourself. That could mean using the timetable on your phone or putting a sticky note nearly you know you'll see.

Secondly, prioritize the money you need to make those minimal payments. However, it can be tempting to dip into that pot, If your bill isn't due for another week. Don't. Missing your minimums only adds to your debt, making your life much harder if a recession hits full force.

You might want to open up a new account with your bank where you specifically store monies for your debt payments If you struggle with this. Once that account is open, transfer what you know you'll need each time you get a stipend.

Paying down credit card debt before a recession

You should prioritize paying it down since credit cards come with more advanced interest rates than most other types of debt If you have credit card debt. The current average credit card interest rate is over 20 percent, and rates are indeed advanced for borrowers with low credit scores. Since credit cards are variable-rate products, the interest rate on your credit card debt is likely to continue rising if the Federal Reserve raises interest rates again as anticipated.

It's worth talking to your credit lender and seeing if you can negotiate a lower interest rate, especially if your credit score has gotten better since you applied for your card. It's also a good idea to write out how important you owe on each credit card and the interest rate and yearly minimum payment for each card. This can help you see the path toward paying off your debt fully or at least making an advanced yearly payment more than the minimum.

It may be worth considering debt connection or working with a debt relief company, If you struggle to make the minimal payments and cannot negotiate with your lender.

Paying down loan debt before a recession

Unlike credit cards, utmost particular and bus loans come with fixed interest rates. This means borrowers who formerly had these loans don't need to worry about their interest rates rising during a recession. However, you should continue, If you have a fixed-rate particular or bus loan and can go to make the yearly payments. If you struggle to make yearly payments, it could be worth looking for a lower-interest product and transferring your debt.

You could talk to a fiscal counsel about transferring your loan debt to a 0 percent APR balance transfer credit card or a home equity line of credit to get a lower interest rate if you have good to excellent credit. You should only do this if you have good credit.

Your stylish option is to rework your budget and prioritize paying down your debt, if you don't have good credit and are upset about being able to pay off a particular or bus loan debt. This is especially important if you have a secured loan so that you don't threaten to lose your auto, home, or other precious means.

What if you can't go to pay off your debt?

Like numerous Americans, are floundering to manage your debt and are upset about the fresh fiscal strain a recession might beget you. However, consider one of the ensuing options, If you're changing it harder and harder to manage debt payments on top of your other charges.

Talk to your lender

It's worth reaching out to your lender to negotiate a temporary payment pause or reduced interest rate If you're passing fiscal difficulty. Some lenders may indeed give relief options during a profitable downturn.

Debt agreement

You'll have to stop paying your creditors while the debt agreement company negotiates with them on your behalf If you decide to work with a debt agreement company. immaculately, your creditors will agree to a lower sum, and you'll establish a payment plan.

A debt agreement is parlous and should only be pursued as a last resort. Your creditors don't have to work with a debt agreement company and could sue you for defaulting on your payments. Also, defaulting on your debt payments will harm your credit score and your capability to adopt monies in the future.

Credit comforting

Consider working with a non-profit credit counselor, If you're floundering with debt and need a professional opinion about your situation. numerous estimable credit comfort agencies will advise you for little to no cost. You can also set up a debt operation plan with these agencies wherein you pay them yearly, and they pay lenders on your behalf. This service simplifies the process for you but requires a fresh yearly figure.

How to budget and save in a recession

Creating and sticking to a budget is essential, but it's indeed more important during a recession. Having one can help you free up cash to put toward your debt.

Below are some ways to produce one.

1. Figure out your yearly charges. Write down your fixed charges, like your rent or mortgage payment, bus payment, and internet bill. also, jot down variable charges, like your average grocery bill. You may have to comb through your billing statements or credit card bills to estimate how important you spend each month on variable charges.

2. Calculate your yearly income. Next, jot down your yearly payment, including what you get paid from any side jobs.

3. Use a spreadsheet or budgeting app. Once you've written down your charges and income, enter this data into a spreadsheet or budgeting app.

4. Trim gratuitous charges. Review your charges to identify what "wants" you can exclude or reduce. For illustration, if you

have an unused yearly subscription to a streaming service, consider canceling it.

5. Deposit a set quantum in a high-yield savings regard. To make an emergency fund, consider depositing a set quantum of any optional income you have into a high-yield savings regard. Doing this can help you avoid taking on debt in the future.

The fastest ways to pay off debt

Nothing wants to be in debt forever. However, you want to get out of it as snappily as possible, if you are like the utmost people. Then are five of the fastest ways to achieve debt freedom

Take advantage of debt relief services

Debt relief services are designed to make it possible for you to pay off your high-interest debts in a reasonable quantum of time without fiscal strain. Debt relief companies generally negotiate this thing in one of three ways

• Debt connection loans Debt connection loans give you a way to pay off multiple high-interest-rate debts with one loan. These loans generally come with low fixed interest rates and fixed payments, making it possible to pay your debts out far more briskly than you would otherwise.

• Debt connection plans Debt collection companies negotiate lower interest rates with your lenders. They'll also produce a fixed payment plan for you. You make a single yearly payment to the debt connection company and the company pays your lenders collectively on your behalf.

• Debt agreement/ concession Eventually, debt agreement companies do not just concentrate on interest rate reductions and fixed payment plans; they also negotiate the quantum of monies you owe on your accounts. Although this option generally leads to the largest savings, it can also have the most mischievous impact on your credit score when compared to debt connection loans and programs. Nevertheless, this is a strong option to put an end to high-interest debt-related fiscal rigors.

Reduce interest where possible

Away from the debt relief options mentioned above, there are a couple of other ways to reduce your interest rates. Those include

• Balance transfer credit cards Balance transfer credit cards frequently offer low promotional interest rates for a predetermined period of time. That could mean you will pay 0 interest for a time or longer. You can transfer high-interest balances to these cards to save money and pay your debts off briskly. Just be sure to make a plan for dealing with an advanced rate once the promotional period expires. That plan could be as simple as taking advantage of another balance transfer credit card or paying all of your debt down before the promotional period ends.

• Call your credit card company if you've been a pious client for a while, a simple phone call to your lender's client service line could lead to a lower rate. Simply ask if you qualify for an interest rate reduction. Be sure to be honest about your fiscal status as well. However, your lender may offer further rate reduction options, if you are facing fiscal difficulty.

Focus on your loftiest interest rate first

High interest rates make it harder to pay off debts. So, when you have redundant monies available, you should use it to make fresh payments on your loftiest-interest debt. It's OK to make minimum payments on the rest of your accounts. Once your loftiest interest rate account is paid off, concentrate on paying off your card with the coming loftiest rate and continue to do so until all of your debts are paid off. This strategy, known as the debt avalanche payment system, could save you significant quantities of time and money in the long run.

Take advantage of openings to earn redundant income

Suppose there are ways you can earn redundant money outside of your day job. For illustration, if you are an artist, consider opening a cell at the original art show to sell your work. This could lead to an alternate income that can help you pay your debts off briskly.

Cut charges where possible

You may also be able to cut your charges. By doing so, you could free up cash to pay your debts off briskly.

"Negotiate with your mileage companies for lower rates," says Brian Martin, Wealth Manager at Merit Financial counsels." frequently, you can communicate with your electric, gas, string, and phone/ internet providers in trouble to lower your yearly rates. In numerous cases, simply informing them of your intent to terminate service or switch to another provider will evoke a lower rate offer."

You could also reduce the number of times you eat at coffs per month, cut the string cord and conclude for streaming services, drink your coffee at home, or take advantage of a putatively endless number of other cost-cutting measures.

How To Manage Your Finances At All Time - **Richard J. Hatcher**

PART FOUR

START INVESTING

What Is Investing? How Can You Start Investing?

Investing is the process of buying that increases in value over time and gives returns in the form of income payments or capital earnings. In a larger sense, investing can also be about spending time or plutocracy to ameliorate your own life or the lives of others. But in the world of finance, investing is the purchase of securities, real estate, and other particulars of value in the pursuit of capital earnings or income.

How Does Investing Work?

In the most straightforward sense, investing works when you buy an asset at a low price and sell it at an advanced price. This kind of return on your investment is called a capital gain. Earning returns by dealing means for a profit — or realizing your capital earnings is one way to make money investing.

When an investment earns in value between when you buy it and when you sell it, it's also known as appreciation.

• A share of stock can be appreciated when a company creates a hot new product that boosts deals, increases the company's earnings, and raises the stock's value on the request.

• A commercial bond could appreciate when it pays 5 periodic interest and the same company issues new bonds that only offer 4 interest, making yours more desirable.

• A commodity like gold might appreciate because the U.S. Bone loses value, driving up demand for gold.

• A home or condo might appreciate in value because you repaired the property, or because the neighborhood became more desirable for youthful families with kiddies.

In addition to gains from capital earnings and appreciation, investing works when you buy and hold means that induce income. rather than realizing capital earnings by dealing with an asset, the thing of income investing is to buy means that induce cash inflow over time and hold on to them without dealing. Numerous stocks pay tips, for illustration. Rather than buying and dealing stocks, tip investors hold stocks and profit from the tip income.

What Are the Introductory Types of Investments?

There are four main asset classes that people can invest in with the expedients of enjoying appreciation: stocks, bonds, goods, and real estate. In addition to these introductory securities, there are finances like collective finances and exchange-traded finances (ETFs) that buy different combinations of these means. When you buy these finances, you're investing hundreds or thousands of individual funds.

Stocks

Companies sell stock to raise monies to fund their business operations. Buying shares of stock gives you partial power over a company and lets you share in its earnings (and the losses). Some stocks also pay tips, which are small regular payments of companies' gains.

Because there are no guaranteed returns and individual companies may go out of business, stocks come with a lesser threat than some other investments.

Bonds

Bonds allow investors to "come to the bank." When companies and countries need to raise capital, they adopt monies from investors by issuing debt, called bonds.

When you invest in bonds, you're lending monies to the issuer for a fixed period of time. In return for your loan, the issuer will pay you a fixed rate of return as well as the money you originally lent them.

Because of their guaranteed, fixed rates of return, bonds are also known as fixed-income investments and are generally less parlous than stocks. Not all bonds are "safe" investments, however. Some bonds are issued by companies with poor credit conditions, meaning they may be more likely to overpass on their prepayment.

Goods

Goods are agrarian products, energy products, and essences, including precious essences. These means are generally the raw accouterments used by assiduity, and their prices depend on request demand. For illustration, if a flood tide impacts the force of wheat, the price of wheat might increase due to failure.

Buying "physical" goods means holding amounts of oil painting, wheat, and gold. As you might imagine, this isn't how most people invest in goods. rather, investors buy goods using futures and options contracts. You can also invest in goods via other securities, like ETFs, or buy the shares of companies that produce goods.

Goods can be fairly high-threat investments. Futures and options investing constantly involve trading with the money you adopt, amplifying your eventuality for losses. That's why buying goods is generally for more educated investors.

Real Estate

You can invest in real estate by buying a home, structure, or a piece of land. Real estate investments vary in threat position and are subject to a wide variety of factors, such as profitable cycles, crime rates, public academy conditions, and original government stability.

People looking to invest in real estate without having to enjoy or manage real estate directly might consider buying shares of a real estate investment trust (REIT). REITs are companies that use real estate to induce income for shareholders. Traditionally, they pay advanced tips more than numerous other means, like stocks.

Collective Finances and ETFs

Collective finances and ETFs invest in stocks, bonds, and goods, following a particular strategy. Finances like ETFs and collective finances let you invest in hundreds or thousands of means as formerly when you buy their shares. This easy diversification makes collective finances and ETFs generally less parlous than individual investments.

While both collective finances and ETFs are types of finances, they operate a little else. collective finances buy and sell a wide range of means and are constantly laboriously managed, meaning an investment professional chooses what they invest in. Collective finances frequently are trying to perform better than a standard indicator. This active, hands-on operation means collective finances generally are more precious to invest in than ETFs.

ETFs also contain hundreds or thousands of individual securities. Rather than trying to beat a particular indicator, ETFs generally try to copy the performance of a particular standard indicator. This unresistant approach to investing means your investment returns will presumably noway exceed average standard performance.

Because they aren't laboriously managed, ETFs generally bring less to invest in than collective finances. Historically, many laboriously managed collective finances have outperformed their standard indicators and unresistant finances long term.

How To understand About Threat and Investing

Different investments come with different situations of threat. Taking on further threat means your investment returns may grow briskly but it also means you face a lesser chance of losing monies. Again, a lower threat means you may earn gains more sluggishly, but your investment is safer.

Deciding how important a threat to take on when investing is called gauging your threat tolerance. However, you presumably have advanced threat forbearance, If you're comfortable with further short-term ups and campo in your investment value for the chance of lesser long-term returns. On the other hand, you might feel more with a slower, more moderate rate of return, with smaller ups and campo. In that case, you may have a lower threat of forbearance.

In general, fiscal counsels recommend you take on further threats when you're investing for a far-out thing, like when young people invest for withdrawal. When you have time and decades before you need your money, you're generally in a better position to recover from dips in your investment value.

For illustration, while the S&P 500 has seen a range of short-term lows, including recessions and depressions, it's still handed average periodic returns of about 10 over the once 100 times. But if you had demanded your money during one of those dips, you might have seen losses. That's why it's important to consider your timeline and overall fiscal situation when investing.

Threat and Diversification

Whatever your threat forbearance, one of the stylish ways to manage threats is to enjoy a variety of different investments. You've presumably heard the saying "Don't put all your eggs in one handbasket. " In the world of investing, this concept is called diversification, and the right position of diversification makes for a successful, well-rounded investment portfolio.

That's how it plays out If stock requests are doing well and gaining steadily, for illustration, it's possible that the corridor of the bond request might be slipping lower. However, you might be losing money — but if you were duly diversified across bond and stock investments, you could limit your losses, If your investments were concentrated in bonds.

By retaining a range of investments, in different companies and different asset classes, you can cushion the losses in one area with the earnings in another. This keeps your portfolio steadily and safely growing over time.

How Can I Start Investing?

Getting started with investing is fairly simple, and you don't need to have a ton of cash. There is how to figure out which kind of freshman investment account is right for you

• If you have a little bit of money to start an account but don't want the burden of picking and choosing investments, you might start investing with a robo-counsel. These are automated investing platforms that help you invest your money in pre-made, diversified portfolios, customized for your threat forbearance and fiscal pretensions.

• If you'd prefer hands-on exploration and choosing your individual investments, you might prefer to open an online brokerage account and hand-pick your own investments. However, flash back to the easy diversification that collective finances and ETFs offer, If you're a freshman.

• If you'd prefer a hands-off approach to investing, with redundant help from a professional, talk to a fiscal counsel who works with new investors. With fiscal counsel, you can make a relationship with a trusted professional who understands your pretensions and can help you both choose and manage your investments over time.

Anyhow of how you choose to start investing, keep in mind that investing is a long-term bid and that You'll reap the topmost benefits by constantly investing over time. That means sticking with an investment strategy whether requests are over or down.

Start Investing Beforehand, and Keep Investing Regularly

"Successful investors generally make wealth totally through regular investments, similar as payroll deductions at work or automatic deductions from a checking or savings regard," says Jess Emery, a prophet for Vanguard finances.

Regularly investing helps you take advantage of natural request oscillations. When you invest a harmonious quantum over time, you buy smaller shares when prices are high and further shares when prices are low.

Good investing begins by investing in yourself. Learn about the types of withdrawal accounts. Get your emergency savings squared down. produce a strategy for paying down your pupil loan debt. And with those crucial fiscal tools in action, you can start investing with confidence — putting the money you have a moment to work securing your future.

KEY NOTES

• Investing involves planting capital (money) toward systems or conditioning that are anticipated to induce a positive return over time.

• The type of returns generated depends on the type of design or asset; real estate can produce both rents and capital earnings; numerous stocks pay daily tips; bonds tend to pay regular interest.

• In investing, threat and return are two sides of the same coin; low threat generally means low anticipated returns, while advanced returns are generally accompanied by advanced threat.

- Investors can take the do-it-yourself approach or employ the services of a professional money director.

- Whether buying security qualifies as investing or enterprise depends on three factors — the quantum of threat taken, the holding period, and the source of returns.

Understanding Investing

Investing is to grow one's plutocracy over time. The anticipation of a positive return in the form of income or price appreciation with statistical significance is the core premise of investing. The diapason of means by which one can invest and earn a return is a veritably wide one.

Threat and return go hand-in-hand in investing; low threat generally means low anticipated returns, while advanced returns are generally accompanied by an advanced threat. At the low-threat end of the diapason are introductory investments similar to instruments of Deposit (CDs); bonds or fixed-income instruments are advanced upon the threat scale, while stocks or equities are regarded as unsafe. Goods and derivations are generally considered to be among the hazardous investments. One can also invest in commodity practical, similar to land or real estate, or delicate particulars, similar to fine art and relics.

Threat and return prospects can vary extensively within the same asset class. For illustration, a blue chip that trades on the New York Stock Exchange will have a veritably different threat-return profile from a micro-cap that trades on a small exchange.

The returns generated by an asset depend on the type of asset. For example, numerous stocks pay daily tips, whereas bonds generally pay interest every quarter. In numerous authorities, different types of income are tested at different rates.

In addition to regular income, similar to a tip or interest, price appreciation is an important element of return. Total return from an investment can therefore be regarded as the sum of income and capital appreciation. Standard & Poor's estimates that since 1926, tips have contributed nearly a third of total equity return for the S&P 500 while capital earnings have contributed two-thirds.1 Capital earnings are thus an important piece of investing.

Economists view investing and saving to be two sides of the same coin. This is because when you save a money by depositing it in a bank, the bank also lends that money to individuals or companies that want to adopt that money to put it to good use.

How to Invest

Do-It-Yourself Investing

The question of" how to invest" boils down to whether you're a Do-it-yourself (DIY) kind of investor or would prefer to have your money managed by a professional. numerous investors who prefer to manage their monies themselves have accounts at reduction or online brokerages because of their low commissions and the ease of executing trades on their platforms.

DIY investing is occasionally called tone-directed investing, and requires a fair quantum of education, skill, time commitment, and the capability to control one's emotions. However, it may be smarter to let a professional help manage your investments, if these attributes don't describe you well.

Professionally- Managed Investing

Investors who prefer professional money operations generally have wealth directors looking after their investments. Wealth directors generally charge their guests a chance of means under operation (AUM) as their freights. While professional money operation is more precious than managing money by oneself, similar investors do not mind paying for the convenience of delegating the exploration, investment decision- timber, and trading to an expert.

A detailed History of Investing

While the conception of investing has been around for glory, investing in its present form can find its roots in the period between the 17th and 18th centuries when the development of the first public requests connected investors with investment openings. The Amsterdam Stock Exchange was established in 1602, and the New York Stock Exchange (NYSE) in 1792.

Industrial Revolution Investing

The Industrial Revolutions of 1760- 1840 and 1860- 1914 redounded in lesser substance as a result of which people amassed savings that could be invested, fostering the development of an advanced banking system. The utmost of the established banks that dominate the investing world began in the 1800s, including Goldman Sachs and J.P. Morgan.

20th Century Investing

The 20th century saw new ground being broken in investment propositions, with the development of new generalities in asset pricing, portfolio proposition, and threat operation. In the latter half of the 20th century, numerous new investment vehicles were introduced, including barricade finances, private equity, adventure capital, REITs, and ETFs.

In the 1990s, the rapid-fire spread of the Internet made online trading and exploration capabilities accessible to the general public, completing the democratization of investing that had commenced further than a century ago.

21st Century Investing

The detonation of thedot.com bubble — a bubble that created a new generation of millionaires from investments in technology-driven and online business stocks steered in the 21st century and maybe set the scene for what was to come. In 2001, the collapse of Enron took center stage, with its full display of fraud that busted the company and its account establishment, Arthur Andersen, as well as numerous of its investors.

One of the most notable events in the 21st century, or history for that matter, is the Great Recession (2007- 2009) when an inviting number of failed investments in mortgage-backed securities crippled husbandry around the world. Well-known banks and investment enterprises went beneath, foreclosures surmounted, and the wealth gap widened.

The 21st century also opened up the world of investing to beginners and unconventional investors by drenching the demand with reduced online investment companies and free-trading apps, similar to Robinhood.

How Can One Start Investing?

You can choose the do-it-yourself route, opting for investments grounded on your investing style, or matriculate with the help of an investment professional, similar to a counsel or broker. Before investing, it's important to determine your preferences and threat forbearance. However, choosing stocks and options, may not be the stylish choice, if threat- antipathetic.

Develop a strategy, outlining how important to invest, how frequently to invest, and what to invest in grounded on pretensions and preferences. Before allocating your coffers, probe the target investment to make it align with your strategy and has the implicit to deliver asked results. Flashback, you do not need a lot of money to begin, and you can modify as your requirements change.

What Are Some Types of Investments?

There are numerous types of investments to choose from. Maybe the most common are stocks, bonds, real estate, and ETFs collective finances. Other types of investments to consider are real estate, CDs, appropriations, cryptocurrencies, goods, collectibles, and precious essences.

How Can Investing Grow My money?

Investing is not reserved for the fat. You can invest in nominal quantities. For illustration, you can buy low-priced stocks, deposit small quantities into an interest-bearing savings account, or save until you accumulate a target quantum to invest. However, similar to a 401 (k), allocate small quantities from your pay until you can increase your investment If your employer offers a withdrawal plan. However, you may realize that your investment has doubled If your employer participates in matching.

You can begin investing in stocks, bonds, and collective finances or indeed open an IRA. Starting with 1,000 is nothing to sneeze at. A $ 1,000 investment in Amazon's IPO in 1997 would yield millions of moments. This was largely due to several stock splits, but it didn't change the result of monumental returns. Savings accounts are available at most fiscal institutions and do not generally bear a large quantum of investment. Savings accounts do not generally boast high- interest rates; so, shop around to find one with the stylish features and utmost competitive rates.

Believe it or not, you can invest in real estate with 1,000. You may not be suitable to buy an income-producing property, but you can invest in a company that does. A real estate investment trust (REIT) is a company that invests in and manages real estate to drive gains and produce income. With 1,000, you can invest in REIT stocks, collective finances, or exchange-traded finances.

Is Investing the Same as Gambling?

No, gambling and investing differ greatly. With investing you put your money to work in systems or conditioning that are anticipated to produce a positive return over time- they've positive anticipated returns. Gambling is to place bets on the issues of events or games. Your money isn't being put to work at all. frequently, gambling has a negative anticipated return. While an investment may lose money, it'll do so because the design involved fails to deliver. The outgrowth of gambling, on the other hand, is due purely to chance.

The nethermost Line

Investing is the act of distributing coffers into commodities to induce income or gain gains. The type of investment you choose might probably depend on what you seek to gain and how sensitive you are to threats. Assuming little threat generally yields lower returns and vice versa for assuming a high threat. Investments can be made in stocks, bonds, real estate, precious essences, and more. Investing can be made with monies, means, cryptocurrency, or other mediums of exchange.

There are different types of investment vehicles, similar to stocks, bonds, collective finances, and real estate, each carrying different situations of pitfalls and prices.

Investors can singly invest without the help of an investment professional or matriculate the services of a certified and registered investment counsel. Technology has also given investors the option of entering automated investment results by way of Robo-advisors.

The quantum of consideration, or money, demanded to invest depends largely on the type of investment and the investor's fiscal position, needs, and pretensions. Numerous vehicles have lowered their minimal investment conditions, allowing more people to share.

Despite how you choose to invest or what you choose to invest in, probe your target, as well as your investment director or platform. Conceivably one of the stylish nuggets of wisdom is from stager and accomplished investor Warren Buffet," no way invest in a business you cannot understand.

PART FIVE

HOW TO BUDGET FOR RETIREMENT

You did it. You worked hard, planned, and set aside money over the times to be suitable to retire. Congratulations! Now, the thing is to remain sheltered. We've talked to dozens of people who didn't plan well, retired, and later had to unretire because they ran out of money. Talk about a letdown!

The key to making sure you have enough saved is to produce a withdrawal budget — and stick to it! Despite what most people suppose, a budget isn't a Grinch. It sets you up for success. It authorizes you to spend. It also brings you peace of mind.

Two to three times before you retire, we suggest you take an honest look at what You'll need to fund your life. produce a budget and try it out for a while. That way, you'll know what adaptations to make. We want you to conjure big. We also want you to be realistic and have a plan to make those dreams a reality!

There are four ways to create your withdrawal budget.

1. Add up your income aqueducts.

We like to suppose your income aqueducts as pails of monies that You'll pull from in withdrawal. Hopefully, you've been investing constantly for times to make wealth in a different set of "pails" that will now come to your stipend!

Sit down with an investment professional and make a list of all of your income aqueducts, like the following

• duty- advantaged withdrawal accounts, like a 401 (k), 403 (b) or Roth IRA.

• Social Security benefits are the icing on the cutlet of your withdrawal fund — not the cutlet itself! We don't want you to count on Uncle Sam to take care of you in withdrawal, but you can calculate your Social Security benefits to know how important it is to anticipate.

• Pensions are a thing of history for numerous Americans, but if you're entering a pension from your employer, get the details from HR.

• Part-time earnings Do you plan to still work then and there in withdrawal? Add up how important you suppose you'll make each time.

• Taxable investments are a way to save for withdrawal, especially if you're a high-income earner. However, you can start to withdraw money during withdrawal, if you've got money put down in a brokerage account.

- Real estate can be a steady source of unresistant income — just make sure you don't carry a single penny of mortgage debt into withdrawal!

- appropriations are an insurance product that numerous people use to fund their withdrawal times.

Total up your projected income grounded on all of these profit aqueducts, also divide that number by how numerous times you plan to live in withdrawal. This is a rough ballpark number for your periodic income. From there, you can break it down into yearly income.

2. Plan your distributions precisely.

Most probably, your 401 (k) or IRAs will be your biggest "pail." When you reach a certain age, you'll begin to take distributions (or withdraw monies) from these accounts. Planning when, how, and from which accounts You'll take distributions is a pivotal part of creating your withdrawal budget.

We can't emphasize how important it is to work with an investment professional as you make these computations. Don't risk a big mistake; your future is too important! An investment pro will help you navigate all the debates about how important to pull out and when to do it.

The main thing is to make sure you're not pulling out so much that you "kill the golden goose" and stop the growth of what you still have invested. In proposition, your portfolio will continue to grow (if you keep it well-balanced in the right collective finances).

3. Have a plan for health care charges.

As you age, you'll notice a lot of new pangs and pains. effects just don't work like they used to! You can anticipate one particular expenditure to increase as you get older — health care. A recent study from Health View services systems found that the average, healthy 65- time-old couple retiring this time will need $ 387,644 to cover health care costs over 20 times! 1 If you divide that number by 20, it adds 19,382 to your periodic charges, or 1,615 each month!

Our stylish piece of advice for health care planning is to talk with an insurance professional. There are many questions an insurance professional will walk you through

• Have you reviewed your health care insurance, and do you understand your content?

• Do you have long-term care insurance in place?

• Have you applied for Medicare?

• Do you have a money set away in an HSA, or are you eligible to open one?

Insurance is complicated. And one sanitarium visit could put you in the hole for a long time! So, make it a priority to meet with an insurance pro!

produce a zero-grounded yearly budget.

A zero-grounded budget helps you spend all your monies on paper and purpose. You used a budget to get to withdrawal, and this budget will help you stay in withdrawal! You no way outgrow the need to plan and track your spending.

What's a zero-grounded budget?

A zero-grounded budget totals up your yearly income and deducts your charges so that nothing is left over. It helps you make sure you're spending, saving, or giving every single bone exactly how you should. You can read further about how to produce a zero-grounded budget but there is a summary of the way

Write down your yearly income (from your "withdrawal pails").

2. Write down your yearly charges.

3. Write down your seasonal charges.

4. Abate your charges from your income to equal zero.

5. Track your spending.

List your yearly charges.

When you're ready to list your charges, start by reviewing your most recent bank statement. Track where your money goes each month. You'll be amazed when you notice all the ways your money leaks out of your bank account.

As you decide how to spend your money, it can be helpful to divide your charges into different orders

Essential charges

- Tithing and charitable paying

- Groceries

- serviceability

- Home form and conservation

- Transportation (gas, auto conservation)

- Clothing

Guess what you don't see on this list is a mortgage payment. You shouldn't carry a single penny of debt into withdrawal — including your mortgage!

Gratuitous Charges

- trip

- Subscription services

- Gymnasiums

- pursuits (especially if you decide to start playing lots of golf in withdrawal!)

- Gift paying (everybody loves those grandbabies!)

- Pet care

Seasonal charges

- Property levies

- Insurance decorations

- bus enrollment

- Christmas, anniversary, birthday, and special occasion spending

Use these orders as a starting point and keep brainstorming until you have a bone quantum for each yearly item.

Start your sinking finances.

You should formerly have an emergency fund in place that will cover three to six months of living charges if the commodity were to be to you. In withdrawal, you'll also want to maintain sinking finances to pay for effects like recesses, Christmas with the grandkids, or new vehicles. Set your sinking fund as a line item in your budget each month and save the money for that particular thing in a high-yield-high-yield savings regard or a money request account.

Manage your spending.

It's not enough to set a budget and stopgap for the best. However, it won't do you any good! Once you produce a yearly budget, you need to work with your partner or a friend who can hold you responsible and keep your cutlet on the palpitation of your spending, If you don't stick to it.

Flashback You're in control of your budget. Be purposeful about the choices you make with money. Tracking your spending will help you stay down from stupidity and stay close to your withdrawal dreams!

Erecting A Budget for Your Spending in Withdrawal

Budgeting your spending in withdrawal aesthetics and works also to the way it does in your working times. You may be faced with new and lesser charges, and having a budget becomes indeed more pivotal to help you live effectively off of your savings. erecting this budget is a step-by-step process.

To calculate your withdrawal budget, it's stylish to first calculate your anticipated average costs per month. As you estimate what your spending in withdrawal might be, it can be easy to underrate your charges. To help avoid being caught short suddenly, start now by making a list of your anticipated costs.

To gauge the delicacy of your read budget, you may want to track your charges for many months to check whether your estimates are aligned with your factual charges. It's also important to realize that your withdrawal budget will change based on when you plan to retire

• If you retire beforehand, say at age 63, you may need a bigger nest egg to carry you through your withdrawal times. You also won't get maximum Social Security benefits. However, you can enjoy the maximum quantum, if you stay until age 70.

• If you retire later, you'll still need to have enough income to last throughout withdrawal, but you'll have smaller times with lower income coming in.

What charges belong in a withdrawal budget?

When estimating your withdrawal budget, consider asking yourself the following questions to help develop a more complete and accurate set of charges

• How much time remains on your mortgage?

• Do you plan to move or reduce your primary hearthstone?

• How will your health insurance decorations change after you retire?

• Have you regarded the increased out-of-fund medical costs that frequently accompany age?

• Do you have all of the insurance you need, or should you budget for fresh decorations, similar to long-term care insurance?

• Will you spend further on trips or pursuits once you have further time to devote to them?

It's important to itemize and classify your anticipated average yearly charges as you plan your withdrawal spending. For illustration, you may have ongoing charges for a specific quantum, but you may also have a fixed expenditure that lasts only a certain number of times, similar to a mortgage.

As you complete your budget planning worksheet, you must also take into consideration your changing income picture. When you turn age 73, You'll have to begin withdrawing needed minimum distributions from utmost withdrawal accounts.

Essential, optional, and one-time withdrawal charges

First, understand what types of charges you're likely to dodge and how big they're going to be each time. This will help you determine the withdrawal income You'll need to meet your average yearly charges as well as cover surprise charges. Your charges may fall into three orders: essential (must-have), optional (voluntary) one-time me (a remarkable but necessary circumstance).

According to the U.S.S. Bureau of Labor Statistics, a ménage run by someone 65 or older spends on average $ 52,141 per time (roughly$ 4,345 a month). 1 How are you going to pay for these charges? Some of your income will presumably appear from fixed sources, similar to Social Security benefits, pensions, and appropriations. But if you're like utmost people, the utmost of your withdrawal income will come from portfolio withdrawals. However, you and your fiscal professional can invest your portfolio to give you the stylish chance at a successful withdrawal, If you know how important withdrawal income You'll need.

• Essential charges

Your essential average yearly charges in withdrawal fall into orders similar to ménage, transportation, living charges, family care, and medical/ health. These are necessary withdrawal charges that you may not be able to live without.

According to the Bureau of Labor Statistics, the average partial yearly breakdown of some of these charges by cost category 1 is 1,573 for casing, $ 597 for transportation, $ 586 for health care, $ 541 for food, and 238 for particular insurance.

• optional charges

• One-time charges

• levies

Putting your budget to work in withdrawal

While it's important to determine your withdrawal budget before you retire, it can be indeed more vital to cover your charges during withdrawal. Because your charges are likely to change over time, you might need to acclimate your withdrawal income plan to reflect these changes. We can help you address your withdrawal enterprises.

By meeting regularly with your fiscal professional during your withdrawal times, you can help ensure that your investment plan continues to meet your requirements as they evolve throughout your continuance.

Factors That Could Lower Your Withdrawal Budget

There's a lot of advice about how to save for withdrawal. But what about when you start to withdraw your savings? Several pitfalls can put a dent in your withdrawal portfolio, but that's where wise withdrawal planning may help.

There are three main pitfalls associated with common profitable factors that could conceivably put a dent in your withdrawal income: request change, low interest rates, and affectation. All three can pose serious pitfalls to your withdrawal security, including your Social Security income. Consider these pitfalls before withdrawing your savings and use informed withdrawal planning to palliate your enterprises.

Stock request change

Though the stock request has historically produced positive returns over the long term, as you near withdrawal, you may want to seek to avoid the threat of request downturns. While it might be tempting to turn fully down from equities to save money, keep in mind that withdrawal can last for decades and you may still need to concentrate on growth. To help cover against volatility, you may want to consider a lower-threat, diversified portfolio that still allows for growth.

Low interest rates

As you near withdrawal, the traditional approach to allocation has been to add further bonds into your portfolio to help reduce the stock request threat. In the moment's low-rate terrain, bonds might not induce enough income on their own. You might consider including equities and real means, like goods or real estate, as part of your withdrawal portfolio to help induce fresh income.

Affectation

The cost of withdrawal is likely to increase over time, which means that your lump-sum savings might not stretch as far as you allowed

. To cover against affectation as an element of your withdrawal planning, you might consider investing a portion of your savings in equities and real means, which are designed to help hedge against this threat. Or, if you're coping with a subvention, you might conclude with one that offers cost-of-living-accelerated payments. Consider these strategies to help offset the threat of affectation.

PART SIX

HOW BEST TO SAVE

A Few Ways How To Save

1. Cancel gratuitous subscription services and enrollments

On your way to getting an effective redeemer, consider getting rid of gratuitous subscriptions. maybe you signed up for a new streaming service for the free promotional period but forgot to cancel it. Or perhaps you have a spa class you no longer use. Go through your yearly credit card or bank statements to look for recreating subscription charges.

You don't need an account at a specific institution to get a helping hand. There are several fintech services like Trim and True bill — that are designed to help you find ways to save on subscriptions and other bills.

2. Automate your savings with an app

Struggling to know how important it is to sock down, try an app that does the work for you If you frequently forget to put money into your savings.

There are a plethora of apps that will automate your savings. Capital and Digit are two options. These automated savings apps are designed to automatically transfer a destined quantum from your stipend into your savings.

You won't earn the loftiest periodic chance yield (or occasionally any) on your deposits with these apps, so once you've saved up a pack, consider transferring the money into a high-yield savings account.

3. Set up automatic payments for bills if you make a steady payment

We're busy. It's all too easy to forget to pay all of our bills on time. One easy way to save money is to pay your bills when they're due, assuming you can go to do so.

Companies charge you late freight for overdue balances. While this might amount to just 5 then or 10 there, those freights snappily add up. Credit card late freights can be a lot more precious.

People with irregular income may want to hold off automating bill payments and rather consider trying a service like Steady, which connects you to side gigs and other earning openings near your payday and bill due dates.

Some banks let you set up a rule within your digital banking account. At Chase Bank, online banking guests can set up a bus- savings rule so that when, for illustration, they admit a$ 1,000 deposit, the bank automatically moves 100 of it into a savings account.

4. Switch banks

Banks induce around 9 billion a time in overdrafts and insufficient finances freight, according to the Consumer Financial Protection Bureau.

It's easy to avoid paying yearly fees, particularly at online banks. Nearly half (45 percent) of checking accounts that don't earn interest are free, according to Bankrate's 2023 checking account and ATM figure study. Some banks will indeed give you a generous perk just for opening an account.

For your savings, look for one that pays a competitive yield. Compare savings account rates and freights to find one that fits your requirements.

5. Open a short-term instrument of deposit (CD)

A one-time CD could help you earn further interest than savings. Plus, a CD's yield is generally fixed; as long as you keep the money in the CD through the duration of the term, you're guaranteed to earn the opening APY. One important caveat: Avoid CDs if you suppose you might need the cash before the CD term ends, so you won't have to pay early pullout penalties.

6. subscribe for prices and fidelity programs

Subscribe up for reduction cards at grocery stores and medicine stores in your area. Using these programs regularly can help you save money at checkout or conceivably help you earn prices toward unborn purchases. Just make sure not to be swayed into buying gratuitous stuff by appealing deals.

7. Buy with cash or set a control on your card

You can trick your brain into saving money every time you go to the store by using cash rather than a credit card to make a purchase. Whatever cash you have is your spending limit. Check out the cash-filling trend to explore this idea further. It's too easy to lose sight of limits with a credit card.

8. Stop paying for convenience

Paying for convenience can save time, but it can bring you money. Taking a little redundant time out of your day to brew your coffee or clean and repair effects around the house can grow your bank account.

Choose to reduce your charges. For illustration, perhaps you value the experience of going to a coffee shop, but you can cut back on how many times you order food delivered to your door.

9. Earn cash back on your purchases

Indeed, when times are toughest, you'll still need to spend money on rudiments, so you might as well be rewarded with a cash reverse. There are cash-reverse credit cards that can help you collect cash back on your purchases. Some don't indeed have a periodic figure.

Your credit card might also have cash-reverse offers at certain retailers, but you might need to conclude in order to redeem this price. These offers may have an expiration date or other terms and conditions, so double-check to ensure you're not caught off guard. Cash-reverse apps might also be an option to consider before you start shopping for new credit cards.

10. Buy in bulk

Buying in bulk, be it at a store or storehouse, can help you save money. But flashback, just because a commodity is vented in bulk doesn't mean it's a good value. Also, only buy particulars in bulk that you suppose You'll use. For example, a veritably large vessel of fop salad might not be a good option for a person living by themselves.

11. Look for tickets and deals

Planning with tickets and checking around for deals can make a major difference. Looking through store pamphlets and online can help you get a good deal and save money. A website extension, similar to Honey's cyber surfed add-on, looks out for pasteboard canons for you.

12. vend unwanted particulars

Sell particulars you don't need for an injection of cash fast.

Look at your closet, garret, garage, or storehouse space to find the dress ring, or hiking thrills you no longer wear. Also, post the item to a popular online business, similar to eBay or Poshmark. A garage trade might be an option for dealing with numerous particulars.

Whatever approach you take, do your schoolwork to avoid regrets. Make sure you know the value of an item before you sell it for lower than it's worth.

13. rethink your casing costs

Casing costs similar to rent or mortgage payments are some of the largest charges in utmost budgets. Moving to a place with a lower rent could help you start saving incontinently. Refinancing your mortgage can help you save money on yearly payments and in the long run. But make sure it makes sense for your situation.

14. Protect around for insurance

Shopping around for insurance can help you save big. occasionally You'll find a better deal as a new client or you can communicate with your insurer to ask them to lower your current rate if it has gone up. speeding insurance products with the same insurance company can also help you save.

15. Limit energy consumption

By reducing how important energy you consume, you're not only helping the terrain but also lowering your yearly bills. Some ways to save money on energy consumption snappily include freeing electronics when they're not in use, switching to LED lightbulbs, and lowering your thermostat a couple of degrees at night during colder months.

16. Downgrade a periodic figure credit card

Occasionally a periodic figure credit card can give real benefits. But it might not make sense to pay this periodic figure if the card discontinues these benefits or if you aren't completely exercising them. Downgrading to a no-periodic-figure card might be a better fit for you if this is an option. Call your issuer to see if you're suitable to downgrade your current card to a no-figure card.

17. Cook your reflections

Food can be a large expenditure in your budget. Prepare for your forthcoming reflections and have a clear understanding of what you need from the grocery store. Make a list, look for tickets, and try not to buy anything that didn't make it on the list. Indeed, without tickets, buying food at a grocery store is significantly less precious than ordering carryout or eating at cafes

18. Try a no-spend day

Not spending any money in a day or week can help you snappily save money. This can force you to think about every bone you spend. After a no-spend day (or days), you may also realize your spending habits have gotten better.

19. Make a budget

Assessing your spending is a way to find areas where you may be wasting money. This can be an eye-opening process. The thing with making a budget is to set a guideline for how important you spend and how much you save each month. It can give you insight into where you can cut down on spending, and it can incentivize you to make savings pretensions.

20. exclude one spending habit moment

There's presumably one treat or convenience that you're paying for on a diurnal or regular basis that you can live without (or indulge in less frequently). Over time, you may get used to skipping this item and it'll no longer be a habit. By following a plan and using some discipline, you can find yourself with further monies at the end of the week or month, and in time, the time.

PART SEVEN

LIVE YOUR DREAM LIFE

Do you have a dream for your life? Are you imagining and working towards the dream life you want to live? Or are you someone who hasn't talked about their dreams in a long time?

You're not alone, if it's been a long time. Only 8 of us fulfill our dreams because too many of us put our dreams on the reverse burner. We put our dreams under the guise of "being too busy" or we mime them off because we are intimately hysterical of failing or being rejected.

So, then the deal is that leaving your dreams by the wayside won't magically stop any time soon unless you decide to pick up your dream and take a different action. It's each in your power. (is not that cool?) Truth: All manifested dreams start with taking one action. And action needs intention.

When you're not living with intention — concentrated on what you want and where you want to go — life will continue to push you around and your dreams will feel further and further down.

But it doesn't have to stay that way. Let me ask you if you had all the courage in the world coupled with all the support, money, and time, how would your life be different?

Now, let me ask it another way if you were not feeling wedged or stagnant, how would you like your life to be different?

Let those questions pound around your heart a bit. Allow yourself to daydream the putatively insolvable. That is an essential step to allowing that seed of a dream to come forth.

Imagine what could be if you allowed that putatively insolvable dream to come possible, at least in your mind, for five twinkles. Sure, you may not know how to make your dream a reality yet — that's what makes it a dream. Yet giving yourself the gift of five twinkles to wonder what your dream life might be like may be the very thing that gives you the courage to take a step toward your dream.

Too numerous of us suppose that featuring was for a youngish interpretation of ourselves or that imagining a dream life is for those who don't understand the "real" world.

Needless to say, my dreams have evolved quite a bit since I was young. And indeed, though they've changed, it does not mean that those remnants of my faded dreams do not still live within me. (I'd still like that gorgeous hubby.)

So yes, it's normal for my dreams to visit me once in a while in my current life. Like the faded scent of your favorite incense, your once dreams may be right there staying for you to either snare them back and start pursuing them or as a fond memory.

Mine occasionally pops up while I am watching a movie or talking to a friend. It does not mean it's a" sign" that I've to achieve those dreams. Some dreams are meant to be what I call" starter dreams;" dreams that begin a trip but may lead you to have a different dream altogether.

I'm now living my dream life (or close enough near to it) indeed though, at present, I am not living any of my" starter dreams." It took me a veritably long time to realize that erecting my dream life was further about how I felt on the inside — about myself, my choices, and my values than external factors, like the size of my house, the aesthetics of a mate, and whether or not

I was a notorious movie star. As I grew in maturity and fearlessness, those external factors started to mean lower once I realized my joy started and ended with esteeming and recognizing — my heart and mind.

You see you and I could have all of our dreams come true. We could "have it all," as they say, but still be miserable if we have not done the internal work demanded to face our fears, love ourselves, and find fulfillment in what we do, whatever that is.

Living your dream life is further than getting every single thing you ever wanted or having your fantasies become reality. It's more extensive than that. And that's good news. The fact that your dream life starts from within means your dream life is fully within your grasp. No matter where you are at the moment, whether you're feeling uninspired, wedged, or crippled by fear (like I was for so long), there are clear ways you can take toward designing, and also living, your dream life!

Do you want to live your dream life? If that answer is yes, let's talk about what it takes to live your dream life, including many misconceptions about living out your dreams.

Dreams Are Attainable

An interpretation of your dream life is attainable. But first, let's get one thing straight, living your dream life does not mean you have to" achieve" anything, similar to becoming a notorious movie star, being the CEO of your million-bone company, marrying Prince Charming, or living in a castle in Spain.

Now, I am not saying achieving is not worthwhile; it can be instigative and comforting. But you and I are both old enough to know that the high of achieving does not last long when it stems from trying to" prove" yourself or" fix" yourself or" run down" from yourself. You will no way feel like you are living your dream life that way indeed if you did achieve all you were seeking. Ever heard about a miserable lottery winner? Exactly.

When you look at your life from an empowered perspective, lead with compassion toward yourself and others, and ensure your particular requirements are met, you'll find all the pieces fall into place. You'll be living your dream life, indeed if it's not that magical movie star life you pictured when you were a sprat. Because you will be happy in your skin, esteem yourself and your opinions, and be recognized to be living the life you have, no matter what it entails.

Now, before I say another thing, I must bandy the difference between fantasies and dreams. Too many of us get confused between the two and ruthlessly beat ourselves up for not achieving what we call a dream, but in reality, it's a fantasy.

Fantasies, all too frequently, feel fully out of our grasp. They feel insolvable, unattainable, indeed silly. Not because we do not want our fantasies or that they cannot come true, but because they can. But fantasies stay fantasies because we are not willing to become the person, we need to be to turn that fantasy into reality.

Or we keep what we intimately want as a fantasy because the fantasy isn't, in our estimation, worth the trouble or life change. Or they're too different from what we are used to, so we don't indeed begin to reach for them. What do I mean by fantasies?

When I was growing up, there was nothing I wanted further than to be the coming Lucille Ball or Carol Burnett. Both women were trailblazing uproarious actresses and super-duper notorious.

I believed if my fantasy came true, getting the coming Lucille Ball, I would eventually feel favored, have loads of cash, and be someone people valued and respected. In other words, I would count. I was convinced that this would heal me from witnessing my parents' terrible deaths and eventually prove my father was wrong about me(he did not like me much).

What made it a fantasy rather than a dream?

First, I did not pursue it. I did not indeed try to figure out how to make it be. It was" that would be nice but." You know the" It would be nice but" feeling, don't you?

For numerous people, fantasies include moving to another country, quitting their job this alternate, or it could be as simple as" I am going to say no to my family from now on." For some people, those conduct feel insolvable or, in other words, a fantasy.

Alternatively, fantasies can have a tincture of make-believe. For case, there was a part of me that did want to make people laugh for a living. But if I was being honest with myself, I wanted to be notorious to escape my life to escape the small city I grew up in, to escape what sounded to be my fate. I can look back at that fantasy with so important clarity now. I wanted so desperately to be different from who I was. If that fantasy came true, my life would be okay. I would be okay. But what I did not know back also — I was formerly okay.

There is nothing wrong with having a fantasy, as long as it does not wisecrack you into believing that if you do not achieve it there is a commodity wrong with you. Dreams, on the other hand, can be big(like being notorious and ridiculous), but they're commodities you have the capability and desire to work towards. Don't let a fantasy trick you into believing none of your dreams can come true. Dreams are a commodity you can work on and make steadily. Living your dream life is within your grasp, just so long as you're willing and open to pursuing it.

Dreams Need Energy

Far too frequently, where our dreams are concerned, we become passengers rather than motorists. We've dreams we may indeed suppose about them frequently but we don't put any trouble into pursuing them. We fall into a cycle of believing our dreams can't come true because day by day, they aren't coming true. And as we continually sit by noticing that our dreams aren't becoming a reality, we get demoralized and put less concentration on them until they're not in the picture presently.

Truth Dreams need work; they bear energy, and not just formally, but every day. That energy can look like hard work being in the inflow or moving forward a bit each day, but that's not all. Dreams bear your passion, drive, joy, and excitement! And what is great about dreams is that is exactly what they give in return. When you devote some passion to your dream life, you'll feel more passion. It's the same with drive, joy, and excitement and you'll admit. So, let's get you back in the motorist's seat. As we always say at Fearless Living, be willing.

Willing to show up for yourself.

Willing to take one action.

Willing to give your dreams a chance at getting a reality.

I can tell you over and over and over again that your dreams can come to a reality, but no advice, guidance, or strategies will do you any good until you choose to be willing.

Dreams Come in All Shapes and Sizes

As we talked about earlier, living your dream life isn't inescapably about getting a movie star, making millions, or living in a castle in Spain. You can begin living your dream life now without any of those external effects once you understand your particular requirements.

What do you need to be happy? What do you need to be fulfilled? What does your ideal life look like? What's most important to you? Now when I bring this up to scholars inside my community called Fearless You, the first time they hear about requirements, they automatically jump to allow about effects that other people need. What do your children need? What do your parents need? What does your partner need? But just like I tell them, as you go through this exercise, it's important to take them out of the equation (just for many twinkles).

This is about YOU. What do YOU need from life to feel fulfilled? Or look at it the other way: What do you need in your life? What drives you up the wall when you don't get it? What do you no longer want to tolerate? Perhaps one of your particular requirements is trust. So anytime your mate bends the verity or your musketeers tell a white taradiddle, you lose it. Perhaps another of your particular requirements is harmony. So, when your siblings begin to dispute yet again or your co-workers just can't see eye-to-eye, you come fully drained and exhausted.

Common particular requirements include (but aren't limited to)

• Belonging

• Trust

- Respect
- Space
- Harmony
- Joy
- fiscal stability
- fellowship
- Church
- Connection
- Love
- Safety

Living your dream life is frequently as simple as determining what your particular requirements are and ensuring they're continually met. Recognizing your requirements is essential for tone- respect because once you claim what your requirements are, you can make changes to your life and life that reflect those requirements. And you can be clear to those around you, especially those you love, about what your requirements are and how important they are to you.

Of course, this is no small feat. But it's vital if you are dying to live your dream life. And honestly, it's more satisfying over the long--term than getting the coming Beyoncé, marrying into the royal family, or copping a $ 10 million manse, indeed though all of those might be instigative and delightful.

Creating a strong foundation by relating your requirements allows you to achieve further than you ever allowed possible because you'll see yourself differently than you do now. That newfound tone- respect, which comes from recognizing your requirements, types amenability to use your voice, uncover clarity of purpose, and have the confidence to achieve your dream life.

Dreams Evolve

Dreams change, grow, and evolve, and that's fully okay (and quite normal!) What you wanted and imagined for yourself when you were youngish, or indeed last week, likely is not the same as what you want for yourself now. (Flashback to the former term I described as" starter dream.")

A changed or evolved dream doesn't mean you have failed or given up on your history tone. It shows growth and tone-mindfulness to be suitable to admit that you want a commodity different from your life now.

WHY IS IT SO TOUGH TO LIVE A LIFE YOU DREAM OF?

Your dreams aren't too big. Your dreams are just not yours

A life that feels complete. A life where we don't rush our morning coffee to get to a place we detest and sit with people we don't like and eat effects that make us shamefaced and repeat the whole cycle while intimately wishing 'I wish had a better life.' Also, some YouTuber or book makes you believe that you can live your dream life. They tell you how their life was just like you and also, they started doing 5 effects and 10 internal shifts and making a gratefulness list and numerous effects like these. And now, look, they're living a dream life.

The external world makes you believe that if you do this and that also your life will change into a dream life. Similar innocent souls as we are, we try to apply everyone's advice. Someone said to wake up at 5 AM and make a gratitude list. Someone said making your bed in the morning can make your life more. While some didn't know you but claimed that you're lazy and should be doing further to achieve further therefore fulfilling your purpose. Maybe, that's where we all went wrong.

Life, I wholeheartedly, believed was supposed to be so simple and sweet. But we made it complicated, undesirable, and tough. Forget about everything for an alternative. And answer these

a) All these vids, books, and podcasts that claim to educate you on 'how to achieve your dream life', do they indeed know the first thing about you?

b) You want to live your dream life but do you indeed know what your dream life looks like? If I ask you to close your eyes and imagine your dream life, will you be able to feel it?

c) What's it in your life right now that you detest so important that you're ready to skip every moment of your life in the race to achieve the perfect interpretation of yourself and your dream life which was vented to you by someone who doesn't know you?

The nethermost line is Life is simple. Life is sweet. Life is beautiful.

But also, the noise of the external world makes you believe that what you're doing isn't enough. Look at you, you have such important potential. However, you can achieve a lot of further effects in life, if you use it and work harder.

And suddenly, what you were doing wasn't enough. You felt the need to do further and achieve further indeed if that meant canceling plans with family and staying in your office for most of your life just to realize 'how little you lived life.'

You spend your youth trying to achieve it all while putting off living for the after part and when you reach that after stage, you don't have as important energy to make unforeseen plans and go hiking, the utmost of your musketeers are dead and the people you love are scattered in the world. So, that after stage is lived with remorse and wishing 'I wish I was 30 so I could do this and that.'

Where did life go in this?

You feel fully satisfied with how you look. Your attention no way goes to external beauty or the comparison of it until the external world tells you that you have uneven skin tone, tanning and you have the nicest features that would look stylish if you use this cream, that oil painting, and the rearmost anti-wrinkle cream.

Also, the same face that was home to horselaugh, joy, and big grins came a graveyard where you mourn to have a brighter skin tone, thinner nose shape, and better teeth until you're 50 and you realize ' You were always perfect and the people who loved no way wanted to see a cute smile or a thin nose, they wanted to see your big smile, hear your jokes and comforting eyes which warms their hearts.

You were fully fine with your life until the noise of the world informed you about 7 other side hustles you can make to make further money and how people of your age are formerly millionaires. And if you aren't by now also you have wasted so much of your life. Now, you and your life become a waste of pieces that you have to work on so you can prove your worth to everyone.

Why Is It Tough?

The reason it's so tough for us to live our dream lives is because ' this dream life ' didn't come from our hearts.

This dream life is a vague idea that's constantly fed to us so that we're always in our chasing mode. The more you stay in chasing mode, the less you suppose, and the more dependent you are on the external world to tell you what you should and shouldn't do.

No wonder, why we've so numerous books on the hacks of productivity. Really? Do you need a book to learn how to be productive? Isn't productivity as simple as getting your burro on your president and putting your head on the work? It's just evidence of how we all are headed toward the same thing while depending on the same people tutoring us on what to do.

How concerning yet so funny.

The reason it's so tough for you to live your dream life is that you're trying to achieve a description that has nothing to do with you. You're just made to believe that if you do this, you'll have that and also, you'll be happier and the value of your life will be advanced.

What Can You Do?

I'm not a monk. I do want to achieve a lot of effects in life. But before, I wanted to have it all so I could prove my worth and make a purposeful life.

I've realized that the worth of my life and myself doesn't depend on how important I achieve. People around me wouldn't give a damn if I make 10k a month of 1k. I'm going to pay my bills. To them, my worth will be further if I laugh with them more and partake in a good virgin- converse now and also.

When you die, people won't talk about your achievements. The world had Albert Einstein and the world had me. Both of us are equal. Because the world moves on. Neither does it remember Albert Einstein every day nor will it flash back to Renuka and not you.

So, all this work you're putting in to make your life and yourself good enough, it's vain. Your physical beauty or colophons of honor the size of your bank account or your aesthetic home is no good for anyone. Sure, it can get your attention for a while. But in the end, no one cares.

If your life doesn't feel satisfying to you indeed after doing it all also you lost the game of life. As I said, I'm not going to ask you to not work to achieve effects. Sure, work hard and make money.

But in the expedients of achieving the perfect description of a dream life, dream body, dream income, and all the more dreams like this, don't forget you have a responsibility towards yourself working on making your life beautiful and particular every day.

It's your job to fill your room with all the effects that make you feel at home and do a little gym at home every weekend, cook good reflections for yourself every evening, belt your favorite tea/ coffee with a good book movie, or just watching the decor out of your window, making plans with your musketeers, calling your parents and telling them how important you love them, soddening your shops, going to bed beforehand and having soft wastes snuggle you. Living your dream life isn't about working every day to stay to get to that ONE FINAL DAY when you'll be able to say 'I did it.'

Living your dream life is about filling your day-to-day life with all the effects that you always wanted to enjoy and idealizing the effects you have. Knowing you can wake up without the solicitude of paying bills and you can start your day as you like and go to work because it helps you to buy your quieting stuff and work with all your fidelity because you know there's further in life which is yet to be unfolded.

You don't have to let go of success to enjoy life or vice versa. You can have both, high intentions and happiness. It's on you.

Whether you want to stay focused on what you can do or take the pressure from the world on 'why are you not doing further?'

The choice is yours. Choose focus. Choose to live your dream life every day rather than staying for that one final day. Don't exhaust your soul. Nourish it with love and joy.

THE END

www.ingramcontent.com/pod-product-compliance
Lightning Source LLC
Chambersburg PA
CBHW071832210526
45479CB00001B/97